¡Las mascotas son geniales!
Pets Are Awesome!

MI HÁMSTER
MY HAMSTER

Norman D. Graubart
Traducción al español: Christina Green

PowerKiDS
press
New York

Published in 2014 by The Rosen Publishing Group, Inc.
29 East 21st Street, New York, NY 10010

First Edition

Book Design: Colleen Bialecki   Traducción al español: Christina Green
Photo Research: Katie Stryker

Photo Credits: Cover Hintau Aliaksei/Shutterstock.com; p. 5 Michelle D. Milliman/Shutterstock.com; p. 7 Alexruss/Shutterstock.com; p. 9 Pyza/Puchikumo/Flickr/Getty Images; p. 11 Alex Kalashnikov/Shutterstock.com; p. 13 Tom Gowamlock/Shutterstock.com; p. 15 VeryOlive/Shutterstock.com; p. 17 Dmitry Noumov/Shutterstock.com; p. 19 Dragan Todorovic/Flickr/Getty Images; p. 21 Khmel Alena/Shutterstock.com; p. 23 Jane September/Shutterstock.com.

Library of Congress Cataloging-in-Publication Data

Graubart, Norman D.
My hamster = Mi hámster / by Norman D. Graubart ; translated by Christina Green. — First edition.
    pages cm. — (Pets are awesome! = ¡Las mascotas son geniales!)
English and Spanish.
Includes index.
ISBN 978-1-4777-3313-4 (library)
1. Hamsters as pets—Juvenile literature. I. Green, Christina, translator. II. Graubart, Norman D. My hamster. III. Graubart, Norman D. My hamster. Spanish. IV. Title. V. Title: Mi hámster.
SF459.H3G72718 2014
636.935'6—dc23
                        2013024247

Web Sites: Due to the changing nature of Internet links, PowerKids Press has developed an online list of websites related to the subject of this book. This site is updated regularly. Please use this link to access the list: www.powerkidslinks.com/paa/hamstr

Manufactured in the United States of America

CPSIA Compliance Information: Batch # W14PK3: For Further Information contact Rosen Publishing, New York, New York at 1-800-237-9932

CONTENIDO

CONTENTS

Los hámsteres son mascotas juguetonas.

_____

Hamsters are playful pets.

4

El **hámster dorado** es el tipo más común de hámster mascota de los Estados Unidos.

Golden hamsters are the most common pet hamsters in the United States.

Los hámsteres pertenecen a la familia de los **roedores**.

Hamsters belong to the **rodent** family.

8

Los hámsteres mascota viven en jaulas o en peceras.

Pet hamsters live in cages or aquariums.

Debes alimentar a tu hámster cada dos o tres días.

You need to feed your hamster every two or three days.

Los hámsteres dorados se descubrieron en Siria.

Golden hamsters were first discovered in Syria.

15

Los hámsteres bebés se llaman **crías**.

Baby hamsters are called **pups**.

¡Los hámsteres tienen
dos estómagos!

Hamsters have two stomachs!

A los hámsteres les encanta correr.

Hamsters love to run.

Si cuidas de tu hámster, él disfrutará jugando contigo.

If you take care of your hamster, it will enjoy playing with you.

22

PALABRAS QUE DEBES SABER
WORDS TO KNOW

(el) hámster dorado
golden hamster

(las) crías
pups

(los) roedores
rodents

ÍNDICE

INDEX

24